Comparing Minibeasts

A World of Minibeasts

Charlotte Guillain

Raintree

www.raintreepublishers.co.uk
Visit our website to find out more information about Raintree books.

To order:
☎ Phone 0845 6044371
🖷 Fax +44 (0) 1865 312263
🖳 Email myorders@raintreepublishers.co.uk

Customers from outside the UK please telephone +44 1865 312262

Raintree is an imprint of Capstone Global Library Limited, a company incorporated in England and Wales having its registered office at 7 Pilgrim Street, London, EC4V 6LB – Registered company number: 6695582

Edited by Daniel Nunn, Rebecca Rissman, and Harriet Milles
Designed by Joanna Hinton-Malivoire
Picture research by Elizabeth Alexander
Originated by Capstone Global Library Ltd.
Production by Victoria Fitzgerald
Printed and bound in China by Leo Paper Products Ltd

ISBN 978 1 406 22894 6 (hardback)
15 14 13 12 11
10 9 8 7 6 5 4 3 2 1

ISBN 978 1 406 22962 2 (paperback)
16 15 14 13 12
10 9 8 7 6 5 4 3 2 1

British Library Cataloguing in Publication Data
Guillain, Charlotte.
  A world of minibeasts. – (Acorn plus)
  1. Insects–Pictorial works–Juvenile literature.
  2. Invertebrates–Pictorial works–Juvenile literature.
  I. Title II. Series
  595.7-dc22
A full catalogue record for this book is available from the British Library.

Acknowledgements
We would like to thank the following for permission to reproduce photographs: Alamy **p. 12** (© blickwinkel); Corbis **p. 21 left** (© Hans Pfletschinger/Science Faction); FLPA **p. 19** (© Michael Durham/Minden Pictures); iStockphoto **p. 18 right** (© Dawn Hudson); Shutterstock **pp. 4 left, 22 bee** (© Daniel Hebert), **4 right, 22 butterfly** (© Leighton Photography & Imaging), **5 left, 22 woodlouse** (© Joseph Calev), **5 right, 9** (© Audrey Snider-Bell), **6, 22 dragonfly** (© iliuta goean), **7 left** (© David Dohnal), **7 right** (© basel101658), **8** (© orionmystery@flickr), **10** (© Dariusz Majgier), **11** (© Wong Hock weng), **13 left & right** (© Cathy Keifer), **14, 22 beetle** (© argonaut), **15 left** (© Chris Mole), **15 right** (© Patrick Power), **16** (© Ariel Bravy), **17** (© Four Oaks), **18 left** (© Vinicius Tupinamba), **20** (© Gregory Guivarch), **21 right, 22 pond skater** (© mjf99).

Front cover photograph of a banana spider and grasshopper on a leaf reproduced with permission of Shutterstock (© Cathy Keifer). Back cover photograph of a dung beetle in South Africa rolling a ball of dung reproduced with permission of Shutterstock (© Four Oaks).

We would like to thank Michael Bright for his invaluable help in the preparation of this book.

Every effort has been made to contact copyright holders of any material reproduced in this book. Any omissions will be rectified in subsequent printings if notice is given to the publisher.

Contents

Some words appear in bold, **like this**. You can find out what they mean in "Words to know" on page 23.

What are minibeasts?

bee

butterfly

Minibeasts are small living things. They do not have **backbones**. There are different types of minibeasts. Some minibeasts are **insects**. Bees and butterflies are insects.

woodlouse

centipede

Not all minibeasts are insects. Spiders, woodlice, centipedes, and worms are other types of minibeasts.

Minibeast bodies

wings

dragonfly

Insects have three main body parts, and six legs. Many insects, such as moths and dragonflies, have wings. Insects' eyes are made of many little eyes next to each other.

wasp

sting

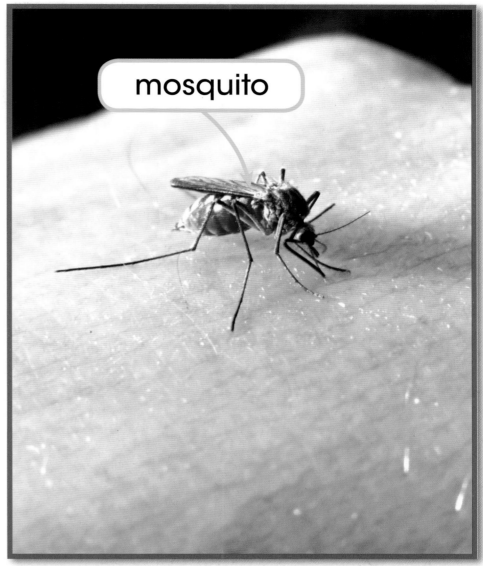

mosquito

Some insects **sting** or bite. Female bees, wasps, and ants have stings. Lice, fleas, and mosquitoes use their mouths to bite, and suck up liquid.

spider

Spiders have eight legs and two body parts. They have six or eight eyes. They have **fangs** to bite. Spiders do not have wings.

antennae

centipede

Centipedes and millipedes have long bodies with many different sections. They have **antennae** and many legs. Centipedes can bite with their claws.

Growing minibeasts

shield bug

eggs

Most minibeasts lay eggs. Centipedes lay eggs in soil. Butterflies, ladybirds, and shield bugs lay eggs on leaves or grass. Mosquitoes lay eggs in water. Spiders wrap their eggs in silk.

eggs

young bugs

Some minibeasts look like their parents when they **hatch**. Young millipedes and centipedes look like small adults. Young grasshoppers and spiders look like small adults, too.

larvae

Not all minibeast babies look like adults. Some eggs **hatch** into **larvae**. Larvae change into **pupae** as they grow. Then they become adults.

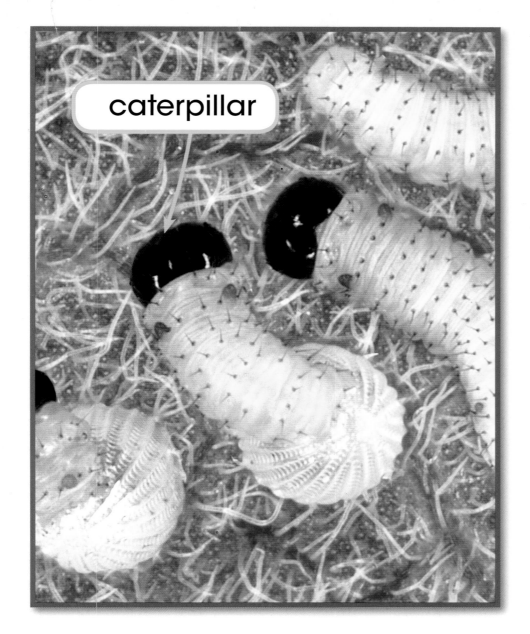

caterpillar

chrysalis

butterfly

A caterpillar is a larva. The caterpillar grows and changes into a pupa called a **chrysalis**. Then it changes into a butterfly inside the chrysalis.

Minibeast homes

beetle

Earthworms, ants, and some centipedes live underground. Many beetles and woodlice live under logs or dead leaves.

web

spider

nest

wasp

Spiders make webs from silk. Bees build nests from **wax**. Some wasps chew things up to make a nest. Other minibeasts live in plants and trees.

Minibeast food

butterfly

Many minibeasts get food from plants. Some minibeasts eat leaves. Bees and butterflies feed on **nectar** from flowers. Other minibeasts eat fruit or seeds.

dung beetle

Some minibeasts eat other minibeasts. Mosquitoes and ticks suck blood. Dung beetles and some flies eat poo. Some big spiders eat mice or birds!

Moving minibeasts

worm

beetle

Many minibeasts run or crawl. Caterpillars, worms, and snails move quite slowly. Ground beetles and spiders move more quickly.

grasshopper

Some minibeasts can jump. Some **insects**, such as grasshoppers, crickets, and fleas, have strong legs to help them jump. Some spiders can jump, too.

hawkmoth

Many **insects** can fly. Hawkmoths fly very quickly. Large beetles fly slowly. Spiders, woodlice, centipedes, and millipedes cannot fly. Spiders can float on the wind.

diving beetle

pond skater

Some insects can swim. Diving beetles paddle with their back legs. Pond skaters move on the top of the water. Water spiders swim underwater.

How big are minibeasts?

These pictures show you how big some of the minibeasts in this book are.

Words to know

antenna feeler on an insect's head. Antennae can be used to feel, taste, and smell.

backbone part of a skeleton that goes from the tail to the head

chrysalis where a caterpillar turns into a butterfly

fangs sharp teeth that can be used to give a poisonous bite. Spiders have fangs.

hatch born from an egg

insect type of minibeast with three body parts and six legs

larvae the young of some types of insect

nectar sweet liquid that is made by flowers

pupae stage in an insect's life cycle between larva and adult

sting part of an insect's body that can give venom

wax sticky substance that bees use to build their nests. Some candles are made from wax.

Index

Notes for parents and teachers

Before reading

Make a list of minibeasts with the children. Try to include insects, arachnids (e.g., spiders), crustacea (e.g., woodlice), myriapods (e.g., centipedes and millipedes) and earthworms, slugs and snails. Ask them what body parts they think each minibeast has. Do they think minibeasts have the same senses as us? Do they know where different minibeasts live, or what they eat?

After reading

• Between spring and late summer you could go on a minibeast hunt. Divide the children into groups and give each group a plastic pot, a paintbrush and a magnifying glass. Go out into the school grounds and look under stones and leaves for minibeasts. Show the children how to gently put any minibeasts they find into the plastic pot using the paint brush and then look at them using a magnifying glass. Emphasize how important it is to treat living creatures carefully and to put them back where they were found. Ask the children to try to identify the minibeasts they find and look at the body parts they have. Tell them to record where they found each minibeast. Share their findings at the end of the hunt.

• Get a butterfly kit for your classroom to watch how caterpillars grow and change into butterflies. Ask the children to make a diary recording how the caterpillars change.

• Get a class wormery to observe what compost worms eat. Discuss how these worms help us to recycle waste and help the environment.